MAD LIBS
WORKBOOK
GRADE 1 READING

written by Wiley Blevins

MAD LIBS
An Imprint of Penguin Random House LLC, New York

Mad Libs format and text copyright © 2020 by Penguin Random House LLC. All rights reserved.

Mad Libs concept created by Roger Price & Leonard Stern

Cover illustration by Scott Brooks
Interior illustrations by Scott Brooks, Tim Haggerty, and Jim Paillot

Designed by Dinardo Design

Published by Mad Libs,
an imprint of Penguin Random House LLC, New York.
Printed in the USA.

Visit us online at www.penguinrandomhouse.com.

ISBN 9780593096154
1 3 5 7 9 10 8 6 4 2

WORKBOOK

— INSTRUCTIONS —

MAD LIBS WORKBOOK is a game for kids who don't like games! It is also a review of the key reading skills for Grade 1. It has both skill practice pages and fun story pages.

RIDICULOUSLY SIMPLE DIRECTIONS:

At the top of each story page, you will find up to four columns of words, each headed by a symbol. Each symbol represents a type of word, such as a noun (naming word) or a verb (action word). The categories and symbols change from story to story. Here's an example:

MAD LIBS WORKBOOK is fun to play by yourself, but you can also play it with friends! To begin, look at the story on the page below. When you come to a blank space in the story, look at the symbol that appears underneath. Then find the same symbol on this page and pick a word that appears below the symbol. Put that word in the blank space, and cross out the word, so you don't use it again. Continue doing this throughout the story until you've filled in all the spaces. Finally, read your story aloud and laugh!

EXAMPLE:

I see a bird. It is _____ and _____ .

The bird lives in a _____ . It is shaped like a _____ .

🐚	🍅	🦋	🦔
green	~~huge~~	school	square
striped	fluffy	~~car~~	triangle
~~polka-dotted~~	skinny	shoe	~~moose~~

I see a bird. It is **polka-dotted** and **huge** .

The bird lives in a **car** . It is shaped like a **moose** .

fat	mat	~~tan~~	crabby
bad	hat	flat	~~lap~~
~~mad~~	~~rat~~	drab	jazz
~~sad~~	bat	~~rad~~	happy

That Cat Sat

MAD _____ cat.

RAD _____ cat.

Cat on a RAT _____.

SAD _____ cat.

TAN _____ cat.

LAP _____ cat sat.

Short i

The **short i** sound can be spelled with the letter **i**.

insect

six

Add **i** to finish each picture name.

p_i_g

w_i_g

k_i_d

l_i_ps

Sight Words

Say each word. Trace it. Say the letter names.

the they do

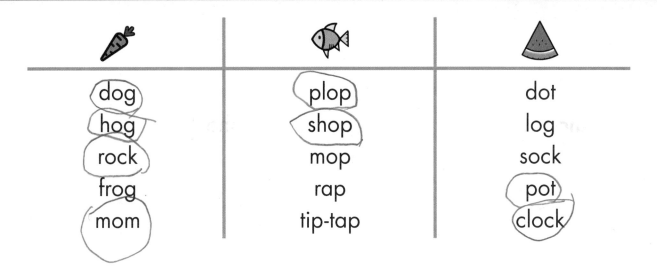

🥕	🐟	🍉
dog	plop	dot
hog	shop	log
rock	mop	sock
frog	rap	pot
mom	tip-tap	clock

Tick-Tock

Tick-tock. The ___rock___ can hop. And my ___dog___ 🥕

can ___shop___ 🐟 on top of a ___clock___ 🍉 .

Tick-tock.

The ___hog___ 🥕 can hop. And my ___mom___ 🥕 can

___plop___ 🐟 on top of a ___pot___ 🍉 .

Tick-tock.

I am *not* a clock. STOP!

Short e

The **short e** sound can be spelled with **e** or **ea**.

red

h**ea**d

Add **e** or **ea** to finish each picture name.

b _e_ d

w _e_ b

l _e_ g

br _e_ _a_ d

Sight Words

Say each word. Trace it. Say the letter names.

to   you   said

🦔	🌴	🍍	🍕
(red hen)	vet	(web)	bed
ten men	van	net	sled
(desk)	(egg)	nest	(cat)
(dog)	tent	cab	mop

Don't Get Wet!

The _desk_ said, "Don't get wet!"
🦔

So, I went to the _egg_ .
🌴

The _dog_ said, "Don't get wet!"
🦔

So, I jumped in the _web_ .
🍍

The _red hen_ said, "Don't get wet!"
🦔

So, I ran under the _cat_ .
🍕

And do you know what?

I got wet!

Short u

The **short u** sound can be spelled with the letter **u**.

up

s**u**n

Add **u** to finish each picture name.

c___p

r___n

j___mp

b___s

Sight Words

Say each word. Trace it. Say the letter names.

see   play   jump

🍦	🌊	❄️	🦆
(bus)	(cup)	cut	bad
(nut)	mud	hug	red
(bug)	jug	tug	(big)
duck	fog	(buzz)	(wet)
(jug)	(pan)	rub	fun

Fun Things to See

Number 1: You can see a __nut__ 🍦 run in

the sun.

Number 2: You can see a __jug__ 🍦

jump in the __pan__ 🌊 .

Number 3: You can see a __big__ 🦆

__bug__ 🍦 sit in a the __cup__ 🌊 .

Number 4: You can see a __wet__ 🦆 fox play with a drum.

Number 5: You can see a __bus__ 🍦 __buzz__ ❄️

a plum. Yum!

Blends

When two consonants are together in a word, we often hear the sound of both letters.

black

stop

Add two letters to finish each picture name.

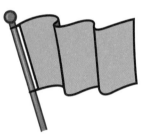

____ ___ag

____ ___im

____ ___ap

____ ___unk

Sight Words

Say each word. Trace it. Say the letter names.

let's   go   one

 👕	🍅	🔺	🐋
black	slug	jumps	sleeps
glass	snake	slips	quacks
flat	fish	skips	swims
slim	blob	flips	scrubs
blue	squid	smells	plops

KATE

Let's Race!

START . . .

Let's go! The race is on.

The _GLASS_ skunk will race the _slim_ 👕
SNAKE 🍅 . Who will win? Let's see.

The skunk takes off. Go, skunk, go! He _FLIPS_ over a log.

He _SMELLS_ 🔺 under a plant. Then he _SKIPS_ 🔺

behind a rock. And what does he do? The skunk _QUACKS_ 🐋

while the _blob_ 🍅 _PLOPS_ 🐋 .

So, who will win?

STOP!

Blends

When two consonants are together in a word, we often hear the sound of both letters.

bridge

dragon

Add two letters to finish each picture name.

___ ___og

___ ___ab

___ ___uck

___ ___ess

Sight Words

Say each word. Trace it. Say the letter names.

friend   good   have

⬤	🍍	🌶️	🍕
Crab	skip	truck	track
Frog	dress	grass	tree
Prince	cry	school	bridge
Bread	clap	box	grill
Grasshopper	growl	crib	house

Dragon's Friends

Dragon has lots of good friends.

____bhed____ is Dragon's friend. They like to

____direrr____ in the ____crib____.

____Grasshopper____ is Dragon's friend, too.

They like to ____grow____ on the

____mon____.

But ____Frog____ is Dragon's best friend. Best friends are

great to have. So, what do they do? They like to ____skip____

by the ____thee____.

Dragon has lots of good friends. Who is your best friend?

Digraphs

When two or more consonants are together in a word, they sometimes make a new sound.

<u>**sh**</u>ip

<u>**ch**</u>eese

wi<u>**tch**</u>

Add **sh**, **ch**, or **tch** to finish each picture name.

___ ___ark

fi___ ___

___ ___oe

___ ___air

___ ___icken

ca___ ___ ___

Sight Words

Say each word. Trace it. Say the letter names.

yes   no   eat

👕	🌴	🍉	🦔
fish	pond	chop	kitchen
chips	dish	switch	shack
ships	shell	catch	grass
dishes	sandwich	push	web
wishes	shoes	wax	puddle

Animal Facts: Yes or No?

1. Sharks like to eat _chips_ 👕 and _dishes_ 👕 .

Yes or no?

2. Fish can swim in a _sanduwich_ 🌴 and a _shoes_ 🌴 .

Yes or no?

3. Chickens like to _____ peaches in the 🍉

_____ . Yes or no? 🦔

4. Dogs like to chase _____ 👕

in the _____ . Yes or no? 🦔

5. Cats like to sleep in the _____ . Yes or no? 🦔

6. Ducks like to _____ bugs. Yes or no? 🍉

Digraphs

When two or more consonants are together in a word, they sometimes make a new sound.

whale

ba**th**

Add **wh** or **th** to finish each picture name.

___ ___ite

$2+2=4$

ma ___ ___

___ ___umb

___ ___eel

── Sight Words ──

Say each word. Trace it. Say the letter names.

who   where   why

		🐶	❄️
A white whale	This week	In the bathtub	fluffy feather
The thin moth	Who is asking?	On a bike path	pink moth
Beth and Ruth	Three o'clock	In math class	chipmunk
A singing king	Thanksgiving	With a friend	bird's nest
The wicked witch	When I said so	While on a bus	bag of bugs

In the News!

Read all about it. It's in the news!

Who? _The wicked witch_

When? _thanksgiving_

Where? _in the bathtub_ 🐶

What? Munched on a

bag of bugs ❄️ and got sick

Why? You tell me.

Read all about it. It's in the news!

Read all about it. It's in the news!

Who? _the thin moth_

When? _This week_

Where? _Was in math class_ 🐶

What? Sat on a _bird's nest_ ❄️

and fell asleep

Why? Who knows?

Read all about it. It's in the news!

Final e

When a word ends in **e**, the vowel before it and the **e** work together to say the vowel's name.

h**o**p

h**o**p**e**

Add a **vowel** (a, e, i, o, u) and **e** (at the end) to finish each picture name.

sm ___ l ___

sn ___ k ___

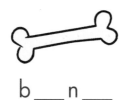

b ___ n ___

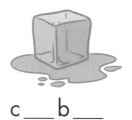

c ___ b ___

Sight Words

Say each word. Trace it. Say the letter names.

one   day   put

👕	🌊	🍦	🦆
snake	ride	lake	grape
(plane)	slide	(stove)	(striped)
mule	(skate)	stone	(broken)
(bone)	date	cave	wide
(nose)	(bite)	(kite)	cute

Save Time?

One day a _bone_ wanted to take a 👕

skate to the _stove_ . 🌊 🍦

She got a _brokin_ backpack and 🦆

filled it with lots of stuff. Then she left home.

On the way, she spotted a _striped nose_ . 🦆 👕

"I will put it in the _kite_ . I can't take it with me," she 🍦

said. "I don't have time."

Then she came across a huge _plehe_ . "I must 👕

bite it," she said. "Oh no! It will make me late. 🌊

How can I save time?" What can she do?

Long a

The **long a** sound can be spelled many ways.

tr**ai**n

pl**ay**

sn**a**k**e**

Add **ai**, **ay**, or **a_e** to finish each picture name.

gr ___ ___

r ___ ___ n

n ___ ___ l

cr ___ ___ on

c ___ k ___

Sight Words

Say each word. Trace it. Say the letter names.

from   or   your

grape	snails	shave	whale
grainy	snakes	lay	tail
hay-like	grapes	bake	cake
drippy	plates	sail	rake
pink	skates	pray	brain

A Rainy Day

It's a rainy day. It is gray and _____ . _____

and _____ fall from the sky. What a day! What

a pain! What will you do? You can stay inside and play.

Or you can _____ in the rain. Hop

on some _____ . You can go see a dancing

_____ . Grab a pan and bake a mud

_____ . You may do what you like with it. You

can sit at home, too. Maybe you will paint your little _____ .

You can also make a _____ _____ .

But as soon as the rain stops, run outside and play! Okay?

Long e

The **long e** sound can be spelled many ways.

str**ee**t

r**ea**d

w**e**

k**e**y

pupp**y**

Add **ee**, **ea**, **e**, **y**, or **ey** to finish each picture name.

l___ ___f

gr___ ___n

monk___ ___

happ___

sh___

Sight Words

Say each word. Spell it out loud. Trace it.

three there they

❄	🍉	🦴	🌴
beach	leaves	green	Eek
tree	cheese	cheap	Whoop-ee
sneeze	bees	sleepy	Puh-leeze
jeep	honey	squeaky	Tweet
strawberry	peas	fuzzy	Mommy

The Three Teeny Pigs

Once upon a time, there lived three teeny pigs. And they made three

teeny homes. Their homes sat on a big _____ . Teeny
❄

Pig 1 made his home out of _____ . Teeny Pig 2 made his
🍉

home out of _____ . Teeny Pig 3 made his home out of
🍉

_____ . One day, a _____ wolf came by. "I will
🍉   🦴

huff and puff and blow your homes down," he said. "Then I will eat you.

Yum!" "_____ !" said Pig 1. "_____ !" said
🌴   🌴

Pig 2. "_____ !" said Pig 3. "In your dreams,"
🌴

they all screamed. And then they chased the wolf

down the street. The end . . . until next week.

Long o

The **long o** sound can be spelled many ways.

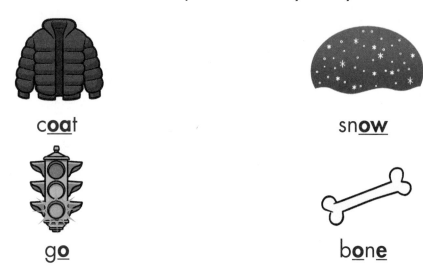

c**oa**t

sn**ow**

g**o**

b**o**n**e**

Add **oa**, **ow**, **o**, or **o_e** to finish each picture name.

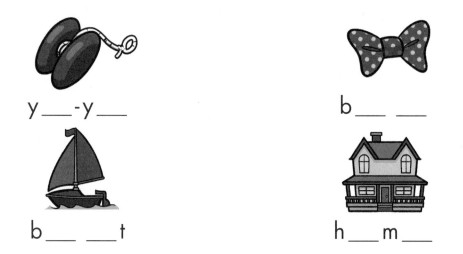

y ___-y ___

b ___ ___

b ___ ___t

h ___ m ___

Sight Words

Say each word. Spell it out loud. Trace it.

many   down   don't

🦋	🍕	🥕	🦔
trolls	goat	snow	throw
moles	coach	road	moan
crows	toad	phone	mow
fish	toast	ghost	float
noses	home	rainbow	groan

Row, Row Your Boat

Many _____ 🦋 like to sing "Row, Row Your

Boat." But can you sing "Row, Row Your

_____ 🍕"? It goes like this.

Row, row your _____ 🍕.

Down, down the stream. Hop in and hold on. Try not to scream.

When you hit the _____ 🥕, hop out and run. Pass by the

_____ 🥕 and _____ 🥕. This is lots of fun! Row,

row, row, and _____ 🦔. Fast around the bend. If the

_____ 🦋 catch you, then help we will send. Go. Go. Go!

Don't be slow. Rowing can get old. But that you already know.

Long i

The **long i** sound can be spelled many ways.

fl**y**   l**igh**t   k**i**nd

sm**i_le**   t**ie**

Add **y**, **igh**, **i**, **i_e**, or **ie** to finish each picture name.

cr ___   n ___ n ___   w ___ ld

p ___ ___   n ___ ___ ___ t

— Sight Words —

Say each word. Spell it out loud. Trace it.

once   upon   time

⊕	🐋	🍦	🍍
flies	pies	shy	fried
bikes	spies	nine	dried
ties	knives	blind	slimed
mice	a child	bright	dined with
sheep	knights	wide	cried with

The Boy Who Cried a Lie

Once upon a time, there lived a boy. He had a big job. He

had to keep a flock of _____ safe at night.
(ball)

Why? _____ or _____ might
(whale)   (whale)

come to eat them. One night, the boy decided to play a

trick. "Help! Help!" he cried. _____ people
(popsicle)

from the town came running. The boy smiled. "What a great

trick!" he said. "You lied," said the people. "Do not try that again."

The next night, the boy fell asleep. _____ came and
(whale)

_____ the flock. "Help! Help!" cried the boy. But no one
(pineapple)

came. That was the end of the flock. And the end of the boy who lied.

Long u

The **long u** sound can be spelled many ways.

f**ew**

m**u**sic

c**u**b**e**

resc**ue**

Add **ew**, **u_e**, **u**, or **ue** to finish each picture name.

men___

f___ ___

c___ t___

arg___ ___

Sight Words

Say each word. Spell it out loud. Trace it.

saw   was   by

🍉	🦴	🧁	🦑
cute	pig	foam	green
music	goat	gold	slime
frog	knight	snakes	rice
maze	crying fly	mice	hay
flea	child	screams	brain

At the Museum

Miss June's class went to a _____ 🍉 museum. They saw a lot

there. They saw a _____ 🦴 shaped like a cube. The cube was

made of _____ 🧁 . They saw a few paintings, too. One had

a _____ 🦴 on it. Another one had a _____ 🦴

on it. It was so cute. By lunchtime, the class was hungry. The museum

had a snack shop. What could the class get to eat? They looked at

the menu. They got _____ 🦑 pie and _____ 🦑

peaches. Just then, the class saw people running.

A painting was on fire. A _____ 🦴 came

to the rescue. What a day at the museum!

r-Controlled Vowels
er, ir, ur

The letters **er**, **ir**, and **ur** all stand for the same sounds.

und**er**

f**ir**st

p**ur**se

Add **er**, **ir**, or **ur** to finish each picture name.

g___ ___l

f___ ___n

p___ ___ple

b___ ___d

Sight Words

Say each word. Spell it out loud. Trace it.

asked   but   cold

🍅	🦢	🍌	🐟
shirts	purred	dirty	turkey
skirts	surfed	purple	jerk
ferns	twirled	nurse	turtle
girls	squirted	circus	germ
birds	hopped	furry	spur

The Ant and the Grasshopper

The days had turned cold. The ants had gathered all the food

they needed for winter. One day, a _____ 🍌

grasshopper _____ by. "I am hungry and thirsty," 🦢

he said. "Why?" asked the ants. "Did you not gather the

_____ and _____ _____ 🍅 🍌 🍅

you need to eat? What did you do all summer? Play?" "Well," said the

grasshopper. "I might be a lazy _____ to you. But I urge 🐟

you to help me." "We only have _____ water for you," 🍌

said the ants. "And some advice. There's a time for work. And a time for

play." And with that, the hungry grasshopper _____ away. 🦢

r-Controlled Vowels or, ar

When a vowel is followed by the letter **r**, the **r** affects the vowel sound. It is neither long nor short.

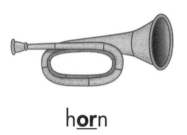

h**or**n

c**ar**

Add **or** or **ar** to finish each picture name.

b___ ___n

c___ ___n

f___ ___k

st___ ___

Sight Words

Say each word. Spell it out loud. Trace it.

with   each   more

🍕	👕	🥕	🏐
pork	dog	barking	sports
beans	goat	roaring	poor
horns	stork	baking	stormy
sharks	door	parking	snoring
scarfs	fork	marching	yarn

On the Farm

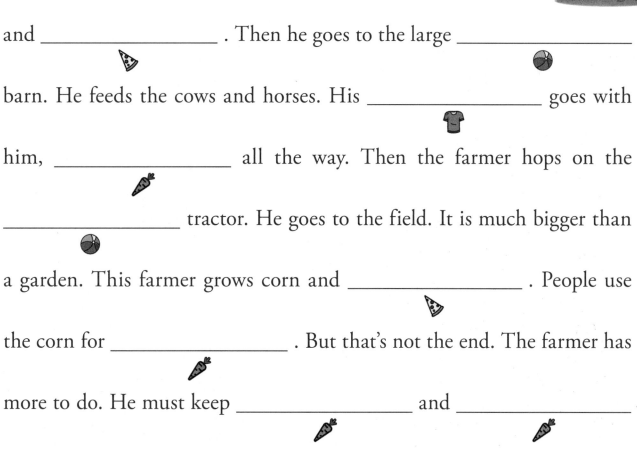

Life on a farm is filled with chores. A farmer must get up

each morning with the sun. He eats a big breakfast of eggs

and _____ 🍕 . Then he goes to the large _____ 🏐

barn. He feeds the cows and horses. His _____ 👕 goes with

him, _____ 🥕 all the way. Then the farmer hops on the

_____ 🏐 tractor. He goes to the field. It is much bigger than

a garden. This farmer grows corn and _____ 🍕 . People use

the corn for _____ 🥕 . But that's not the end. The farmer has

more to do. He must keep _____ 🥕 and _____ 🥕

before it gets dark. And the next day it starts all over again!

Diphthongs oi, oy; ou, ow

Some vowel sounds feel like they move around in your mouth.

b**oy**

s**oi**l

m**ou**th

d**ow**n

Add **oy**, **oi**, **ou**, or **ow** to finish each picture name.

b___ ___l

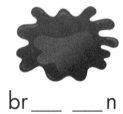

h___ ___se

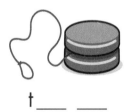

t___ ___

br___ ___n

Sight Words

Say each word. Spell it out loud. Trace it.

things   make   me

🦔	🦋	🍅	🍦
clown	loud	gown	growl
flower	brown	cloud	snout
mouse	moist	mouth	pouch
cowboy	sour	toy	frown
house	joyful	towel	couch

Shout It Out!

Lots of things make me shout. An owl with a screeching

howl. A noisy boy. But what makes you shout?

1. Does a _____ in a _____
🦔   🍅

make you shout? Then shout it out!

2. Does a _____ with a _____
🦔   🍦

make you shout? Then shout it out!

3. If you saw a _____ _____ , would you
🦋   🍅

shout? Then shout it out!

4. What about a _____ _____ , would you
🦋   🍦

shout now? Then shout it out! (But not too loud.)

Variant Vowels oo

The letters **oo** stand for two different sounds.
These sounds can be spelled many ways.

b**oo**k   m**oo**n   gl**ue**

gr**ou**p   n**ew**   J**u**n**e**

Add **oo**, **ue**, or **ou** to finish each picture name.

w___ ___d   br___ ___m   bl___ ___

h___ ___d   s___ ___p   f___ ___d

Sight Words

Say each word. Spell it out loud. Trace it.

be   is   what

🌴	🐋	🦴	🍉
smooth	mushroom	cookies	a school
blue	broom	boots	a pool
wooden	tooth	prunes	a bathroom
rude	goose	kangaroos	a book
new	foot	balloons	shampoo

Clues

Here's a clue. What do you do?

There's only one rule. Read it.

What is bright at night? It looks

like a _____ .
🐋

Answer: It is the moon.

What can you eat with a spoon?

It is made of _____
🌴

_____ and a
🦴

_____ .
🐋

Answer: It is soup.

What makes things stick? It can

be in _____ . You
🍉

can find it in _____ .
🍉

Answer: It is glue.

What is filled with

_____
🦴

and new _____ ?
🦴

You can sleep and play there.

Answer: It is your bedroom.

Variant Vowels au, aw, al

The vowel sound in **all** can be spelled many ways.

h**aw**k   s**au**sage   b**all**

t**al**k   s**al**t

Add **aw**, **au**, or **al** to finish each picture name.

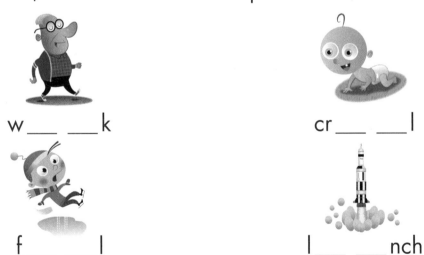

w___ ___k   cr___ ___l

f___ ___l   l___ ___nch

— Sight Words —

Say each word. Spell it out loud. Trace it.

all   come   lived

🌊 seahorse	🌶️ chili	👕 shirt	❄️ snowflake
sausage	crawl to	small	chalk
slaw	draw	tall	strawberries
hawks	squawk at	awful	salt
astronauts	yawn with	awesome	sauce
lawyers	talk to	straw	laundry

Dinosaurs in Space

Dinosaurs come in all shapes and sizes. They walked on Earth long

ago. But what if dinosaurs lived in space? What would that be like?

What would the _____ dinosaurs eat? They might eat
👕

_____ with a side of _____ . Or they
🌊   ❄️

could eat _____ on a bed of _____ .
🌊   ❄️

Yum! What would the _____ dinosaurs do? They might
👕

_____ a friend on a sunny day. Or
🌶️

they might _____ you! What fun!
🌶️

That's what I think it would be like if dinosaurs

lived in space.

WRITING: Spelling and Grammar

Plurals s, es

A **plural** word is more than one of something.
One dog. Two dogs.
Most naming words, or nouns, add **s** to make them plural.
You add **es** when the word ends in **x**, **s**, **ss**, **ch**, or **sh**.

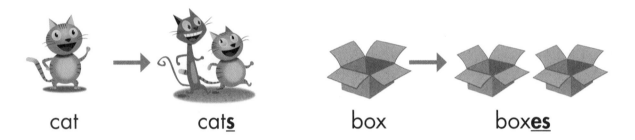

cat   cat**s**   box   box**es**

Add **s** or **es** to finish each picture name.

pig_____

dish_____

car_____

bus_____

peach_____

dress_____

fox_____

hat_____

── Sight Words ──

Say each word. Trace it. Say the letter names.

this   too   every

⚪	🐟	🍌	🧁
goats	clucked	frogs	swam
cowboys	slept	clowns	hopped
foxes	drew	classes	wiggled
buses	fainted	coaches	raced
kangaroos	sang	sandwiches	burped

One Too Many

Once there lived a man, his wife, and ten kids.

"This house is too full!" shouted the man. The next

day, two _____ came to visit. They
      ⚪

_____ all around the house. The day after that, three
  🐟

_____ came to visit. They _____ in every
  ⚪   🐟

room. After that, four _____ and five _____
      🍌   🍌

came to visit. They _____ all day and night. The man ran
  🐟

to his neighbor. "What can I do?" he cried. "Tell everyone the visit is over,"

said the neighbor. The next day, everyone _____ home. All
      🧁

that was left was the man, his wife, and his kids. And that felt just right.

Inflectional Ending ed

You can add the ending **ed** to a verb, or action word.
It makes the verb past tense.
That means the action already happened.

cook

cook**ed**

Add **ed** to each word. Write a sentence using that word.

walk___ ___: _____

call___ ___: _____

start___ ___: _____

Sight Words

Say each word. Trace it. Say the letter names.

first   we   blue

marched	zoo	ate	pickle
zoomed	store	smelled	poodle
crawled	pool	walked on	turtle
jumped	farm	washed	sock
screamed	school	lifted	frog

Yesterday: A Checklist

Yesterday, I did many things. It's hard to remember them all.

But my checklist helps!

✔ First, I _____ to the _____ with my
🍍 🐶

friends. We _____ cake and a _____ .
🥕 🍕

✔ Next, I _____ to the _____ with my
🍍 🐶

mom and dad. We _____ a dirty _____ .
🥕 🍕

We do this every week. We all love it.

✔ At last, I _____ with my dog. We _____ a
🍍 🥕

_____ . It was blue and purple. That was so much fun!
🍕

What did you do yesterday?

Inflectional Endings
s, ed, ing

You can add **s**, **ed**, or **ing** to a verb, or action word.

| paint | paint**s** | paint**ed** | paint**ing** |

Add **s**, **ed**, and **ing** to each word.
Say a sentence for each word.

	Add **s**	Add **ed**	Add **ing**
ask	_____	_____	_____
clean	_____	_____	_____
stomp	_____	_____	_____

Sight Words

Say each word. Trace it. Say the letter names.

so also different

🍌	🍕	🍦	🍅
cleaned	boxing	barn	rubber
marched	licking	kitchen	green
talked	singing	bathroom	sad
played	sleeping	pool	mini
camped	laughing	car	hairless

Yesterday or Today?

What do you do every day? Each day is different for me. Yesterday,

I _____ with my _____ kitten. We also
        🍌   🍅

_____ in the _____ . After that, we
        🍌   🍦

_____ in the _____ .
        🍌   🍦

We just had to. It was so much fun! You should try it.

Today is a slow day for me. I am _____
                                        🍕

with my _____ puppy. I am also _____ in
                🍅   🍕

the _____ . I'm thinking about _____ in the
        🍦   🍕

_____ , too. My friends will join in the fun.
        🍦

What will I do tomorrow? It's a surprise! What will you do?

WRITING: Spelling and Grammar

Inflectional Endings with Spelling Changes

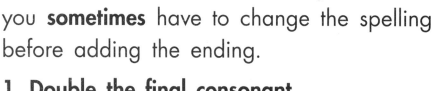

When you add **s**, **es**, **ed**, or **ing** to a word, you **sometimes** have to change the spelling before adding the ending.

1. Double the final consonant

| hop | hops | ho**pp**ed | ho**pp**ing |

2. Drop e

| save | saves | saved | sav**ing** |

3. Change y to i

| try | tr**i**es | tr**i**ed | trying |

Add **s**, **ed**, and **ing** to each word.
Say a sentence for each word.

	Add **s** or **es**	Add **ed**	Add **ing**
stop	_____	_____	_____
bake	_____	_____	_____
cry	_____	_____	_____

Sight Words

Say each word. Trace it. Say the letter names.

other   school   people

❄	🌴	🏐	🐋
cat	ship	wet	sing
poodle	cup	cold	cook
carrot	barn	large	sleep
nose	pool	pink	dance
spoon	tree	cracked	sneeze

Be Brave

Firefighters have a big job. They must be brave, too. I once saw a

firefighter on the job. He saved a _____ from a burning
                                          ❄

_____ . He also saved a _____
        🌴   ❄

that was stuck in a _____ . Then, he grabbed a
                            🌴

_____ _____ and put out the blaze.
        🏐   ❄

Other workers must be brave, too. A bus driver must

_____ on the bus. Kids get to school faster that way.
        🐋

A police officer must _____ on the job, too.
                              🐋

That keeps people safe and happy. Which workers do you

think are brave? Why?

Nouns

A **noun** is a naming word.
A person, place, or thing is a noun.

Person	Place	Thing

girl	**school**	**flower**

Add a noun to finish each sentence.

The _____ ran fast!

Did you go to the _____?

I see a _____ in my yard.

Sight Words

Say each word. Trace it. Say the letter names.

here   know   laugh

🦄	🍅	🦋	🦔
kid	bite	store	sad
fish	smile	zoo	singing
shark	dance	sea	flat
teacher	read	parade	tired
snail	bark	White House	wiggly

It's a Fact

A fact is something that is true. Here are some facts I just learned.

Are they really true? It's a fact that a _____

_____ can _____ .
   🦄   🍅

I saw it on TV. My dog barked, then fainted.

It's a fact that a _____ _____ can
           🦔   🦄

_____ . I saw it once at the _____ .
 🍅   🦋

My mom screamed. My dad cried. And my little sister laughed.

It's a fact that a _____ _____ can
           🦔   🦄

_____ . I saw it at the _____ . It was
 🍅   🦋

dark and raining. So it was quite a shock! What fun facts do you know?

Verbs

A **verb** is an action word.
Every sentence must have a verb.

run

hop

Add a verb to finish each sentence.

I can _____ !

Can you _____ ?

The dog likes to _____ .

I like to _____ .

Sight Words

Say each word. Trace it. Say the letter names.

can   above   while

🍍	🐟	🥕	🦢
dance	rock	hide	truck
sing	box	spit	kitten
sleep	school	spin	shark
cook	hat	bathe	baby
flop	bus	giggle	bear

Let's Do This!

Can you or can't you? Take the challenge.

Can you _____ on top of a
🍍

_____ ? I can. I bet you can, too! Can you
🐟

_____ under a _____ ? I can. I bet you
🍍 🐟

can, too! Can you _____ inside a _____ ?
🍍 🐟

I can. I bet you can, too! Now let's try something harder. Can you

_____ with a _____ ? I can. I bet you can,
🥕 🦢

too! Can you _____ above a _____ ? I can.
🥕 🦢

I bet you can, too! Can you _____ while chewing gum?
🥕

Well . . . I can't. You win!

Pronouns

A **pronoun** takes the place of a noun.

I, **you**, **he**, **she**, **it**, **we**, and **they** are pronouns.

<u>Noun</u>   <u>Pronoun</u>

The **man** ran in the park.   **He** ran in the park.

Add a pronoun to finish each sentence.

The girl sleeps.   _____ sleeps.

The flower is pretty.   _____ is pretty.

The kids are loud!   _____ are loud!

─── Sight Words ───

Say each word. Trace it. Say the letter names.

his   find   two

🧁	🦴	🍉	🌊
forest	tree	sat	witch
school	ant	hid	mermaid
bathroom	pea	slept	unicorn
city	ghost	cried	princess

Hansel and Gretel

Once upon a time, Hansel and Gretel got lost in the BATHROOM 🧁 .

"We must find help," said Hansel. He took his sister's hand. "I can lead

the way," Gretel said. She walked beside a large TREE 🦴 . Then

she CRIED 🍉 behind a/an GHOST 🦴 . At last, they came

to the home of a UNICORN 🌊 . She was waiting for them. "Come

in, my sweets," she said. Hansel spotted a large ANT 🦴 . He

began to shake. Gretel grabbed him. The two tugged on the door. It was

stuck. Just then, Gretel spotted a WITCH 🌊 .

"Help!" she yelled. And she and Hansel ran all the way

to the CITY 🧁 . THE END

WRITING: Spelling and Grammar

Adjectives

An **adjective** is a describing word.
It tells more about something.

a dog

a **big** dog

a **brown** dog

Add adjectives to finish each sentence.

The _____ frog hops.

The flower is _____ .

The _____ boy has a/an _____ hat.

Sight Words

Say each word. Trace it. Say the letter names.

are   big   when

👕	🌶️	🐶	🍡
pig	paint	pink	skinny
horse	dance	fluffy	rusty
duck	sing	spotted	grumpy
dinosaur	dribble	gold	crying
unicorn	cook	hairless	ticklish

Animal Farm

My uncle lives on a big farm. An animal farm. But the animals on this

farm are a bit different. For example, he has a _____

_____ . It can _____ . Really! It likes
   👕　　　　　　　　　　　　🌶️

to do that with the cow. This cow is _____ and
   🐶

_____ . It can also _____
   🍡　　　　　　　　　　　　🌶️

when it's happy. I saw it one night. I couldn't believe

my eyes. Then there is the _____
   🍡

_____ . When no one is watching,
   👕

it will _____ on a table.
   🌶️

My uncle has the best farm ever!

Conjunctions

A **conjunction** is a word that joins words or parts of sentences.

They are like glue words.

The words **and**, **but**, and **or** are conjunctions.

Max **and** Maria like to swim.

Do you like apples **or** peaches?

I like apples, **but** I don't like grapes.

Add **and**, **but**, or **or** to finish each sentence.

We read _____ write at school.

Tim likes to run, _____ Jeff likes to swim.

Do you want to eat pizza _____ burgers for lunch?

Sight Words

Say each word. Trace it. Say the letter names.

sure   wasn't   please

🏐	🥕	🦔	🍍
mouse	beach	police	rat
moose	box	clowns	rabbit
man	bike	mayor	rake
marble	bank	hamsters	rainbow
mirror	barn	bees	roof

And the Story Goes On

Max told Maria that a _____ 🏐 and a _____ 🍍

went to a _____ 🥕 . Well, Maria told Lin that a

_____ 🏐 or a _____ 🍍 ran

in a _____ 🥕 . She wasn't sure. Next,

Lin told her sister that a _____ 🏐

fell into a _____ 🥕 , but the _____ 🍍 did not.

Her sister got scared. So she told her mom that a _____ 🏐

and a _____ 🍍 were coming to eat them. Mom called the

_____ 🦔 and the _____ 🦔 . They came and said

one thing: "Please stop talking!"

Prepositions

Prepositions tell more about a noun or verb in a sentence. Some prepositions are **above**, **across**, **after**, **around**, **at**, **before**, **behind**, **beside**, **beyond**, **by**, **down**, **during**, **for**, **from**, **in**, **into**, **near**, **of**, **on**, **over**, **to**, **under**, and **with**.

<u>Tells More About a Noun</u>
The food **on** the table is hot.

<u>Tells More About a Verb</u>
We walk **to** school.

Add a preposition to finish each sentence.

We went _____ the store.

The dog sat _____ the tree.

The park is _____ my house.

── Sight Words ──

Say each word. Trace it. Say the letter names.

its   doing   want

🐋	🐶	🌊	🍕
~~under~~	belly	~~pickle~~	box
behind	~~face~~	~~mouse~~	clown
~~on top of~~	friend	car	~~elephant~~
~~inside~~	~~nose~~	spider	~~fly~~
near	dog	~~teacher~~	~~house~~

Where Is It?

Where is the cat? It is __INSIDE__ the rug. What is it doing? 🐋

It is licking its fuzzy __NOSE__ . Slurp, slurp, slurp! 🐶

Where is the green __TEACHER__ ? It is __ONTOPOF__ the 🌊 🐋

__HOUSE__ . Can you see it? It is eating its __FACE__ . 🍕 🐶

Yum, yum, yum! Where is the __MOUSE__ ? It is 🌊

__UNDER__ the __ELEPHANT__ . Don't 🐋 🍕

look now. It is chasing a __PICKLE__ . 🌊

Will it catch it? Do you want it to?

I certainly do, do, do!

Capitalization

What begins with a capital letter?

- the first word in a sentence
- the word **I**
- the name of an exact person or place

The cat sat.

I can read.

My best friend's name is **Maria**.

Fix each sentence.

dad and i made a cake.

_____

the farm has lots of cows.

_____

Sight Words

Say each word. Trace it. Say the letter names.

story   today   through

🌴	🍉	🧁
Mrs. Snail	goat	broom
Dr. Shots	fish	flea
Mr. Stinky	bee	wig
Miss Fizz	giraffe	friend
Bob	hippo	socks

Mr. Smith's Class

I am in Mr. Smith's first-grade class. Today, we had a

lot of visitors. First came _____ . They
🌴

showed us their new _____ . Next,
🧁

_____ came. They helped us make a
🌴

robot _____ . After that, a _____ flew into
🧁 🍉

the window. The odd thing is, it started to talk. Then it read us a story.

Finally, a _____ marched through the door. We played tag
🍉

in the classroom. Well, it was chasing us with a _____ .
🧁

But it felt like tag. What a fun day in Mr. Smith's first-grade class. I

wonder who will visit tomorrow!

End Punctuation

. A telling sentence ends with a period.

? A question sentence ends with a question mark.

! A sentence showing great excitement ends with an exclamation mark.

The bugs are red and black**.**

Where is my book**?**

I am so hot**!**

Add an end mark to each sentence.

What is your favorite book____
Watch out for that big snake____
I go to school____

Sight Words

Say each word. Trace it. Say the letter names.

walk   found   even

❄	🍌	🏐	👕
rat	fuzzy	tree	EEK!
boat	purple	bear	Rats!
clown	flat	leaf	Oh no!
rock	sticky	cloud	Pickles!
banana	smelly	ear	Mercy!

Why Are You Yelling?!

One day I was walking through the park. I saw a big hairy

_____ . It was really, really gross! So, I showed it to my
❄

sister. "_____" she screamed. That was fun. What did
👕

I find next? Under a rock, I spotted a _____ . It was
❄

_____ and _____ . Wow! What should I
🍌 🍌

do with it? I showed it to my sister, of course. "_____"
👕

she screamed. That was fun. What did I find next? I found my sister.

She was hiding behind a/an _____ .
🏐

"_____" I screamed and fainted.
👕

"That was fun," she said. Now we're even!

WRITING: Spelling and Grammar

Commas in a Series

You use a comma (,) to separate three or more words in a series.

I like to run, swim, and play soccer.

Add commas to these sentences.

We ate bread cheese and nuts.

I see dogs cats and rabbits.

Mom Dad and I went shopping.

Sight Words

Say each word. Trace it. Say the letter names.

family   like   buy

🍍	🐟	🦴	🌶️
toy	jelly	nails	paper
star	soup	wood	pens
dollar	pickles	seeds	books
baby	soap	gum	ties
bubble	ice	leaves	glue

Going to the Store

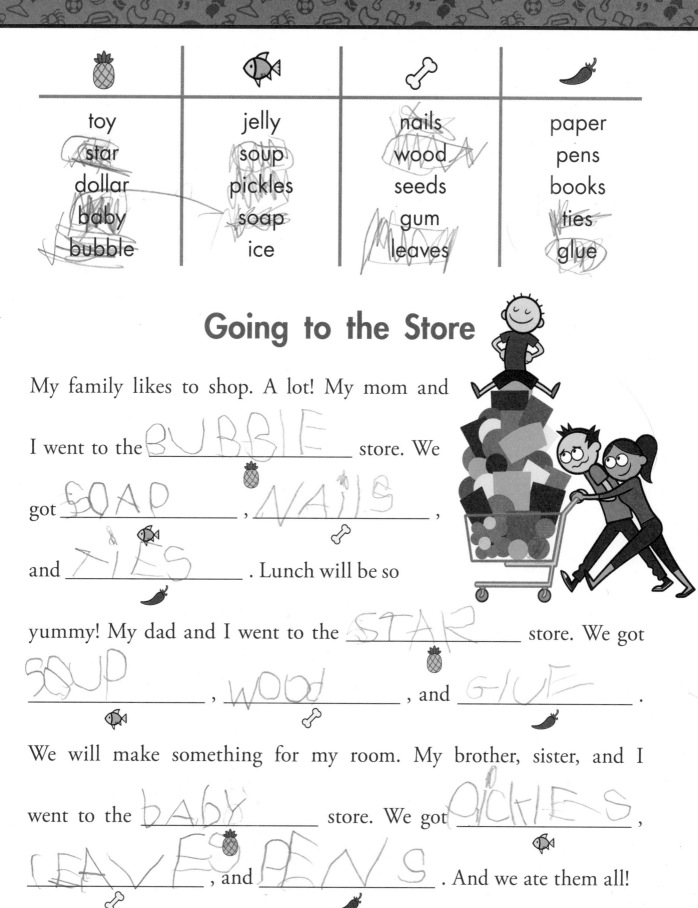

My family likes to shop. A lot! My mom and

I went to the _BUBBLE_ store. We

got _SOAP_ 🍍 , _NAILS_ 🦴 ,

and _TIES_ 🌶️ . Lunch will be so

yummy! My dad and I went to the _STAR_ 🍍 store. We got

SOUP 🐟 , _WOOD_ 🦴 , and _GLUE_ 🌶️ .

We will make something for my room. My brother, sister, and I

went to the _BABY_ 🍍 store. We got _PICKLES_ 🐟 ,

LEAVES 🦴 , and _PENS_ 🌶️ . And we ate them all!

Do you shop with your family? Where do you go? What do you buy?

Contractions

A **contraction** is a shortened way to write two words. The letter or letters left out when putting together the two words are replaced by an apostrophe (').

I am = I'm   do not = don't

I have = I've   we will = we'll

he is = he's   let us = let's

Write the contraction for each word pair.

is not _____   they will _____

we have _____   she is _____

did not _____   are not _____

she will _____   there is _____

Sight Words

Say each word. Trace it. Say the letter names.

some   which   just

🍦	🐶	🍉	🍌
fly	eat	chair	raining
elephant	sleep	dog	snowing
tractor	sing	cow	snoring
baby	play	bubble	bathing
bird	dance	cactus	jumping

I Just Can't

Some things many people can do. But other things are

hard. Which things can or can't you do?

"I can't _____ with my

_____," said the loud

_____ . "I just can't. Can you?"

"That's not bad," said the short _____ . "I can't

_____ on a _____ . I just can't. Can you?"

"You two have it easy," said the skinny _____ . "That isn't

hard. I can't _____ when it's _____ or I'm

_____ . I just can't! Can you?"

Compound Words

Compound words are two or more words that together make a new word.

Often the meanings of the smaller words can help you figure out the meaning of the longer word.

snow + man = snowman

rain + bow = rainbow

Write the compound word.

sun + light _____

dog + house _____

cup + cake _____

bath + tub _____

Draw a picture of one of the words.

Sight Words

Say each word. Trace it. Say the letter names.

their   our   after

🦋	🌴	🦛
baseball	goldfish	basketball
butterfly	bullfrogs	teacup
snowman	jellyfish	raincoat
cupcake	pancakes	toenail
popcorn	scarecrows	ladybug

Fun in the Park

My friends and I went to the park. We were going to play

_____ . But we ran into a _____ team.
     🦋   🦋

"Come play with us," they said. Their team wasn't like ours. They had

two _____ . They had three _____ . And
     🌴   🌴

they had four _____ . Could we beat them? I grabbed
           🌴

the _____ and ran. The other team's
   🦛

players chased me. They couldn't catch me. So,

they grabbed a _____ and threw
              🦛

it at me. Plop! I tumbled to the ground. But not

before I scored a point!

Prefixes

A **prefix** is a word part added to the beginning of a word. It changes the meaning of the word.

happy	**un**happy	(not happy)
read	**re**read	(read again)

Add **un** or **re** to finish each word.

_____tie   _____do

_____make   _____able

─────── Sight Words ───────

Say each word. Trace it. Say the letter names.

about   done   work

🌴	🍦	🦴	🌶️
bunnies	troll	eat	trash
rocks	goldfish	lick	bath
grass	princess	rip	bus
frogs	bean	color	zoo
fleas	chair	smell	tree

School Tips

1. You read a book about _____ . What do you do?
🌴

Always reread the book. Then give it to a _____ .
🍦

2. You are done with your work. What do you do? Review it. Then

_____ it or put it in the _____ .
🦴   🌶️

3. You don't like to retie your shoes in gym class? What do you do?

Wear _____ on your feet.
🌴

4. You are unhappy about your friends. What do you do?

Bring a _____ to school. Eat lunch
🍦

together. Then play in the _____ .
🌶️

Sensory Words

Words that describe things using our five senses are called **sensory words**.

Touch I feel _____ .

Smell I smell _____ .

Sight I see _____ .

Sound I hear _____ .

Taste I taste _____ .

Add a sensory word to describe each thing.

The cake _____ good.   I _____ a skunk.

I _____ loud noises.   The blanket _____ soft.

Sight Words

Say each word. Trace it. Say the letter names.

went   then   yesterday

🍕	🦔	🐟	🏀
frog	furry	leaf	chicken
witch	green	bird	cheese
rock	little	elf	boogers
nose	gooey	bear	clouds
car	bubbly	fly	pickles

On My Walk

I went on a walk yesterday.

I went to the woods.

I saw a _____ _____ .
              🦔   🍕

I heard a _____ _____ .
            🦔   🍕

I touched a _____ _____ .
          🦔   🐟

I smelled a _____ _____ .
         🦔   🐟

Then I ate it.

It tasted like _____ .
       🏀

I went on a walk yesterday.

I went to the woods.

Shades of Meaning: Verbs

Verbs are action words. Some verbs mean almost the same thing. However, each verb has a slightly different meaning.

whisper   (talk quietly)

talk   (talk normally)

shout   (talk loudly)

Add a verb to finish each sentence: **ate**, **nibbled**, **gobbled**.

I _____ my lunch. It was very good.

I _____ down the cake. I was so hungry!

I _____ on a piece of bread. I wasn't very hungry.

Sight Words

Say each word. Trace it. Say the letter names.

he's   for   must

🌊 (seahorse)	👕 (shirt)	🍅 (tomato)	🐶 (dog)
robot	pencils	eat	purple
skunk	slime	slurp	silver
bird	pebbles	gobble	huge
crayon	blood	gulp	smelly
leaf	frogs	chow on	happy

Our Sub

My teacher was sick today. So Mr. Sub was our sub. He's a

_____ (dog) _____ (seahorse) . He had some odd rules for us.

1. You must write with a _____ (dog) _____ (seahorse) .

2. At lunch, you must _____ (tomato) _____ (shirt) on

toast. Then drink a glass of _____ (shirt) .

3. At recess, you must _____ (tomato) dirt and seesaws.

4. After recess, you must read. It has to be a book

about a _____ (seahorse) .

Well, there is only one thing we really must do.

Get a new sub!

Shades of Meaning: Verbs

Verbs are action words. Some verbs mean almost the same thing. However, each verb has a slightly different meaning.

walk

skip

march

Add a verb to finish each sentence: **looked**, **stared**, **peeked**.

I _____ at the cat. It was black and cute.

I _____ at that mean dog! I was scared to look away.

I _____ around the corner. I didn't want to be seen.

Sight Words

Say each word. Trace it. Say the letter names.

over   well   year

🦆	🍌	❄️	🍅
water	march	bikes	cry
glitter	trot	cows	scream
purple	run	drums	bark
little	skip	books	squeak
bubble	roll	horns	sing

Fourth of July Parade

It's the Fourth of July. We will have a big parade in town.

_____ bands will play their _____ . Bam!

🦆   ❄️

Bam! Bang! The bands will _____ up and down the

🍌

street. Next will come the clowns. They will _____ on

🍌

_____ _____ . Kids will _____

🦆   ❄️   🍅

and _____ . All the people will _____

🍌   🍅

when it's over. That's what will happen at the big parade. Well . . . that's

what happened last year.

Shades of Meaning: Adjectives

Adjectives are describing words. Some adjectives mean almost the same thing. However, each adjective has a slightly different meaning.

big

huge (very big)

Add an adjective to finish each sentence: **little**, **tiny**.

I see a _____ kitten. It is so cute!

Can you find the _____ pin? I can't see it.

Sight Words

Say each word. Trace it. Say the letter names.

away   out   think

🧁	🦋	🍍	🐳
tickle	worms	large	little
lick	socks	huge	tiny
sniff	leaves	giant	mini
sneeze on	glitter	jumbo	wee
crush	foil	husky	dinky

The Lion and the Mouse

One day, a _____ mouse met a
🍍

_____ lion. "I will _____
🐳   🧁

you," said the lion. ROAR! The mouse let out

a _____ laugh. "If you try,
🍍

I will _____ you," he said. Then he sped
🧁

away. Days passed. The mouse went out for a walk. He heard a

_____ cry. "What is that?" he asked. He looked and
🐳

found the lion. He was wrapped in _____ .
🦋

"Help me," cried the lion. "Hmm," said the mouse.

"Should I? What do you think?"

Shades of Meaning: Adjectives

Adjectives are describing words. Some adjectives mean almost the same thing. However, each adjective has a slightly different meaning.

cold

freezing (very cold)

Add an adjective to finish each sentence: **pretty**, **beautiful**.

The butterfly is _____ .

That is the most _____ butterfly in the world!

Sight Words

Say each word. Trace it. Say the letter names.

in   pretty   favorite

🥕	🦔	🍉	🍡
burning	icy	bacon	snowballs
sizzling	freezing	butterflies	bubbles
baking	cold	boys	cheese
boiling	frosty	bugs	flies
scorching	chilly	boogers	Santa

Hot or Cold?

In summer, it is _____ hot.
🥕

Like _____ on a _____ pan.
🍉   🥕

Like _____ sitting on the _____ sun.
🍉   🥕

Like _____ after a _____ bath.
🍉   🥕

In winter, it is _____ .
🦔

Like _____ stuck in the _____ fridge.
🍡   🦔

Like _____ walking in the _____ snow.
🍡   🦔

Like _____ sitting on a/an _____ ice cube.
🍡   🦔

Which season is your favorite?

Word Categories

Some words have things in common.
We can put these words in the same group, or category.

Clothing Words

coat
hat
dress
shoe

Fill in the chart.

Food Words

Sight Words

Say each word. Trace it. Say the letter names.

always   made   really

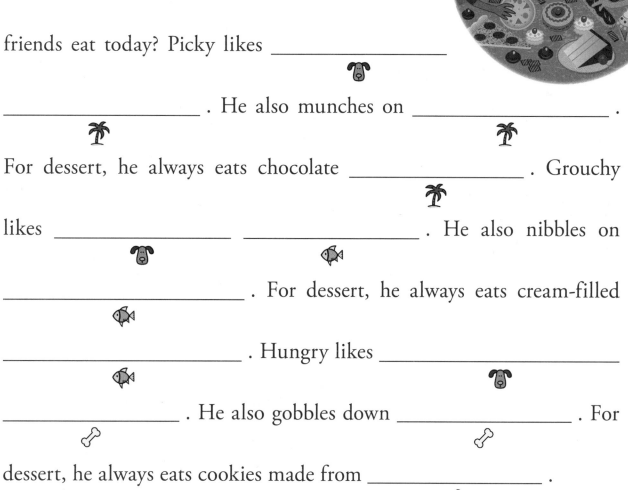 🌴	🐶	🐟	🦴
worms	glue	horses	shoes
bugs	booger	geese	hats
spiders	slime	eagles	pants
ants	mud	lions	socks
fleas	dirty	cats	buttons

Time for Lunch

My friends really like to eat. Sweet things. Sour

things. Things with sauce. So what will my

friends eat today? Picky likes _____
🐶

_____ . He also munches on _____ .
🌴

For dessert, he always eats chocolate _____ . Grouchy
🌴

likes _____ _____ . He also nibbles on
🐶   🐟

_____ . For dessert, he always eats cream-filled
🐟

_____ . Hungry likes _____
🐟   🐶

_____ . He also gobbles down _____ . For
🦴   🦴

dessert, he always eats cookies made from _____ .
🦴

Word Categories

Some words have things in common.
We can put these words in the same group, or category.

Animal Words
bear
mouse
cat
snake

Fill in the chart.

Color Words

Sight Words

Say each word. Trace it. Say the letter names.

any   head   special

🍅	🦋	🍍	🍌
puppy	purple	rough	spotted
fly	brown	smooth	striped
frog	gold	bubbled	bendy
pig	green	hairy	sticky
moose	teal	wet	glowing

Rainbow of Animals

Our town's zoo is special. We have a rainbow of animals. Start at the

zoo's gate. You will find a _____ _____ .
🦋 🍅

It can flip and flop. Such fun! Next, head to the pond. You will find

a _____ and _____ _____ .
🦋 🍌 🍅

It likes to wave to the crowd. After that, go to the big cages. You will

find a _____ _____ . It growls as loud as
🍍 🍅

a bus horn. Finally, visit the zoo's lunchroom. Outside, you will find

a _____ and _____
🍍 🍌

_____ . It will gobble down any
🍅

extra food you have.

ANSWER KEY

---

6 | **PHONICS**

Short a

The **short a** sound can be spelled with the letter **a**.

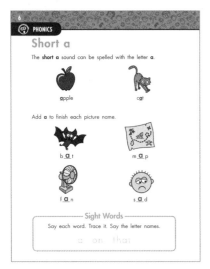

apple   cat

Add **a** to finish each picture name.

b**a**t   m**a**p

f**a**n   s**a**d

— Sight Words —

Say each word. Trace it. Say the letter names.

a on that

---

8 | **PHONICS**

Short i

The **short i** sound can be spelled with the letter **i**.

insect   six

Add **i** to finish each picture name.

p**i**g   w**i**g

k**i**d   l**i**ps

— Sight Words —

Say each word. Trace it. Say the letter names.

the they do

---

10 | **PHONICS**

Short o

The **short o** sound can be spelled with the letter **o**.

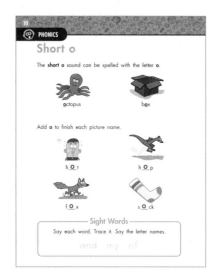

octopus   box

Add **o** to finish each picture name.

h**o**t   h**o**p

f**o**x   s**o**ck

— Sight Words —

Say each word. Trace it. Say the letter names.

and my of

---

12 | **PHONICS**

Short e

The **short e** sound can be spelled with **e** or **ea**.

red   head

Add **e** or **ea** to finish each picture name.

b**e**d   w**e**b

l**e**g   br**ea**d

— Sight Words —

Say each word. Trace it. Say the letter names.

to you said

---

14 | **PHONICS**

Short u

The **short u** sound can be spelled with the letter **u**.

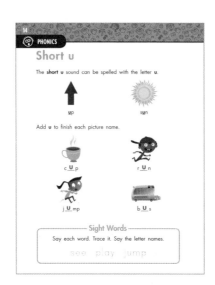

up   sun

Add **u** to finish each picture name.

c**u**p   r**u**n

j**u**mp   b**u**s

— Sight Words —

Say each word. Trace it. Say the letter names.

see play jump

---

16 | **PHONICS**

Blends

When two consonants are together in a word, we often hear the sound of both letters.

black   stop

Add two letters to finish each picture name.

f**l**ag   s**w**im

c**l**ap   s**k**unk

— Sight Words —

Say each word. Trace it. Say the letter names.

let's go one

---

18 | **PHONICS**

Blends

When two consonants are together in a word, we often hear the sound of both letters.

bridge   dragon

Add two letters to finish each picture name.

f**r**og   c**r**ab

t**r**uck   d**r**ess

— Sight Words —

Say each word. Trace it. Say the letter names.

friend good have

---

20 | **PHONICS**

Digraphs

When two or more consonants are together in a word, they sometimes make a new sound.

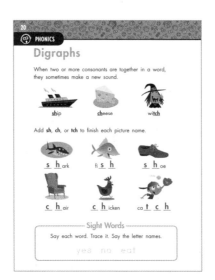

ship   cheese   witch

Add **sh**, **ch**, or **tch** to finish each picture name.

s**h**ark   fi**sh**   s**h**oe

c**h**air   c**h**icken   ca**tch**

— Sight Words —

Say each word. Trace it. Say the letter names.

yes no eat

---

22 | **PHONICS**

Digraphs

When two or more consonants are together in a word, they sometimes make a new sound.

whale   both

Add **wh** or **th** to finish each picture name.

w**h**ite   ma**th**   2+2=4

t**h**umb   w**h**eel

— Sight Words —

Say each word. Trace it. Say the letter names.

who where why

24 PHONICS

Final e

When a word ends in **e**, the vowel before it and the **e** work together to say the vowel's name.

hop   hope

Add a **vowel** (a, e, i, o, u) and **e** (at the end) to finish each picture name.

sm **i** l **e**   sn **a** k **e**

b **o** n **e**   c **u** b **e**

— Sight Words —
Say each word. Trace it. Say the letter names.

one day put

26 PHONICS

Long a

The **long a** sound can be spelled many ways.

train   play   snake

Add **ai**, **ay**, or **a_e** to finish each picture name.

gr **a y**   r **a i** n   n **a i** l

cr **a y** on   c **a** k **e**

— Sight Words —
Say each word. Trace it. Say the letter names.

from or your

28 PHONICS

Long e

The **long e** sound can be spelled many ways.

street   read   we

key   puppy

Add **ee**, **ea**, **y**, or **ey** to finish each picture name.

l e **a** f   gr **e e** n   monk **e y**

happ **y**   sh **e**

— Sight Words —
Say each word. Spell it out loud. Trace it.

three there they

30 PHONICS

Long o

The **long o** sound can be spelled many ways.

coat   snow

go   bone

Add **oa**, **ow**, **o**, or **o_e** to finish each picture name.

y **o**-y **o**   b **o w**

b **o a** t   h **o** m **e**

— Sight Words —
Say each word. Spell it out loud. Trace it.

many down don't

32 PHONICS

Long i

The **long i** sound can be spelled many ways.

fly   light   kind

smile   tie

Add **y**, **igh**, **i_e**, or **ie** to finish each picture name.

cr **y**   n **i** n **e**   w **i** ld

p **ie**   n **igh** t

— Sight Words —
Say each word. Spell it out loud. Trace it.

once upon time

34 PHONICS

Long u

The **long u** sound can be spelled many ways.

few   cube

music   rescue

Add **ew**, **u_e**, **u**, or **ue** to finish each picture name.

men **u**   c **u** t **e**

f **ew**   arg **u e**

— Sight Words —
Say each word. Spell it out loud. Trace it.

saw was by

36 PHONICS

r-Controlled Vowels er, ir, ur

The letters **er**, **ir**, and **ur** all stand for the same sounds.

under   first   purse

Add **er**, **ir**, or **ur** to finish each picture name.

g **i r** l   f e **r** n

p **u r** ple   b **i r** d

— Sight Words —
Say each word. Spell it out loud. Trace it.

asked but cold

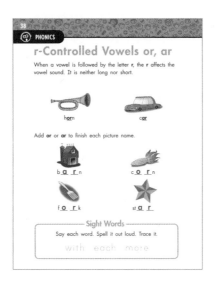

38 PHONICS

r-Controlled Vowels or, ar

When a vowel is followed by the letter **r**, the **r** affects the vowel sound. It is neither long nor short.

horn   car

Add **or** or **ar** to finish each picture name.

b **ar** n   c **or** n

f **or** k   st **ar**

— Sight Words —
Say each word. Spell it out loud. Trace it.

with each more

40 PHONICS

Diphthongs oi, oy; ou, ow

Some vowel sounds feel like they move around in your mouth.

boy   soil

mouth   down

Add **oy**, **oi**, **ou**, or **ow** to finish each picture name.

b **oi** l   h **ou** se

t **oy**   br **ow** n

— Sight Words —
Say each word. Spell it out loud. Trace it.

things make me

94

 **ANSWER KEY**

42 PHONICS
Variant Vowels oo
The letters **oo** stand for two different sounds. These sounds can be spelled many ways.

book · moon · glue
group · new · June

Add **oo**, **ue**, or **ou** to finish each picture name.

w**oo**d · br**oo**m · bl**ue**
h**oo**d · s**ou**p · f**oo**d

Sight Words
Say each word. Spell it out loud. Trace it.
be is what

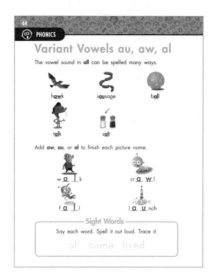

44 PHONICS
Variant Vowels au, aw, al
The vowel sound in **all** can be spelled many ways.

hawk · sausage · ball
talk · salt

Add **aw**, **au**, or **al** to finish each picture name.

w**al**k · cr**aw**l
f**al**l · l**au**nch

Sight Words
Say each word. Spell it out loud. Trace it.
all come lived

46 WRITING: Spelling and Grammar
Plurals s, es
A **plural** word is more than one of something. One dog. Two dogs. Most naming words, or nouns, add **s** to make them plural. You add **es** when the word ends in **x, s, ss, ch,** or **sh**.

cat → cat**s** · box → box**es**

Add **s** or **es** to finish each picture name.

pig **s** · peach **es**
dish **es** · dress **es**
car **s** · fox **es**
bus **es** · hat **s**

Sight Words
Say each word. Trace it. Say the letter names.
this too every

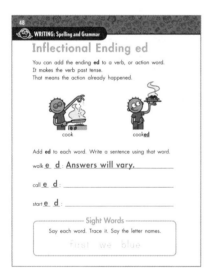

48 WRITING: Spelling and Grammar
Inflectional Ending ed
You can add the ending **ed** to a verb, or action word. It makes the verb past tense. That means the action already happened.

cook · cook**ed**

Add **ed** to each word. Write a sentence using that word.

walk **e d** : Answers will vary.
call **e d** :
start **e d** :

Sight Words
Say each word. Trace it. Say the letter names.
first we blue

50 WRITING: Spelling and Grammar
Inflectional Endings s, ed, ing
You can add **s, ed,** or **ing** to a verb, or action word.

paint · paint**s** · paint**ed** · paint**ing**

Add **s, ed,** and **ing** to each word. Say a sentence for each word.

	Add s	Add ed	Add ing
ask	asks	asked	asking
clean	cleans	cleaned	cleaning
stomp	stomps	stomped	stomping

Sight Words
Say each word. Trace it. Say the letter names.
so also different

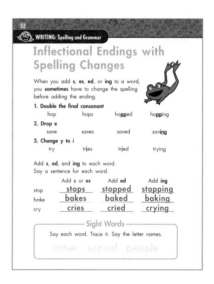

52 WRITING: Spelling and Grammar
Inflectional Endings with Spelling Changes
When you add **s, es, ed,** or **ing** to a word, you **sometimes** have to change the spelling before adding the ending.

1. Double the final consonant
hop · hops · hopped · hopping
2. Drop e
save · saves · saved · saving
3. Change y to i
try · tries · tried · trying

Add **s, ed,** and **ing** to each word. Say a sentence for each word.

	Add s or es	Add ed	Add ing
stop	stops	stopped	stopping
bake	bakes	baked	baking
cry	cries	cried	crying

Sight Words
Say each word. Trace it. Say the letter names.
other school people

54 WRITING: Spelling and Grammar
Nouns
A **noun** is a naming word. A person, place, or thing is a noun.

Person · Place · Thing
girl · school · flower

Add a noun to finish each sentence.
Answers will vary.
The _____ ran fast!
Did you go to the _____?
I see a _____ in my yard.

Sight Words
Say each word. Trace it. Say the letter names.
here know laugh

56 WRITING: Spelling and Grammar
Verbs
A **verb** is an action word. Every sentence must have a verb.

run · hop

Add a verb to finish each sentence.
Answers will vary.
I can _____!
Can you _____?
The dog likes to _____.
I like to _____.

Sight Words
Say each word. Trace it. Say the letter names.
can above while

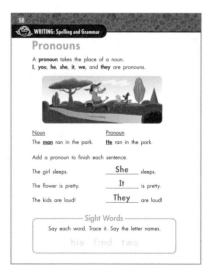

58 WRITING: Spelling and Grammar
Pronouns
A **pronoun** takes the place of a noun. **I, you, he, she, it, we,** and **they** are pronouns.

Noun	Pronoun
The **man** ran in the park.	**He** ran in the park.

Add a pronoun to finish each sentence.
The girl sleeps. **She** sleeps.
The flower is pretty. **It** is pretty.
The kids are loud! **They** are loud!

Sight Words
Say each word. Trace it. Say the letter names.
his find two

60 WRITING: Spelling and Grammar
Adjectives

An **adjective** is a describing word.
It tells more about something.

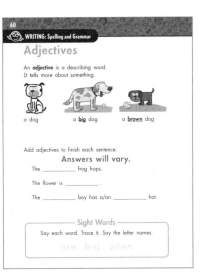

a dog   a **big** dog   a **brown** dog

Add adjectives to finish each sentence.
Answers will vary.
The _____ frog hops.
The flower is _____ .
The _____ boy has a/an _____ hat.

— Sight Words —
Say each word. Trace it. Say the letter names.
are   big   when

62 WRITING: Spelling and Grammar
Conjunctions

A **conjunction** is a word that joins words or parts of sentences.
They are like glue words.
The words **and**, **but**, and **or** are conjunctions.

Max **and** Maria like to swim.
Do you like apples **or** peaches?
I like apples, **but** I don't like grapes.

Add **and**, **but**, or **or** to finish each sentence.
We read __and__ write at school.
Tim likes to run, __but__ Jeff likes to swim.
Do you want to eat pizza __or__ burgers for lunch?

— Sight Words —
Say each word. Trace it. Say the letter names.
are   wasn't   please

64 WRITING: Spelling and Grammar
Prepositions

Prepositions tell more about a noun or verb in a sentence.
Some prepositions are **above, across, after, around, at, before, behind, beside, beyond, by, down, during, for, from, in, into, near, of, on, over, to, under,** and **with.**

Tells More About a Noun
The food **on** the table is hot.

Tells More About a Verb
We walk **to** school.

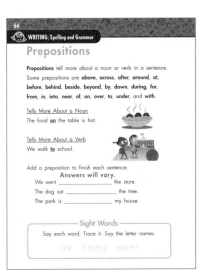

Add a preposition to finish each sentence.
Answers will vary.
We went _____ the store.
The dog sat _____ the tree.
The park is _____ my house.

— Sight Words —
Say each word. Trace it. Say the letter names.
its   doing   want

66 WRITING: Spelling and Grammar
Capitalization

What begins with a capital letter?
• the first word in a sentence
• the word **I**
• the name of an exact person or place

The cat sat.
I can read.
My best friend's name is **Maria**.

Fix each sentence.
dad and i made a cake.
Dad and I made a cake.
the farm has lots of cows.
The farm has lots of cows.

— Sight Words —
Say each word. Trace it. Say the letter names.
story   today   through

68 WRITING: Spelling and Grammar
End Punctuation

. A telling sentence ends with a period.
? A question sentence ends with a question mark.
! A sentence showing great excitement ends with an exclamation mark.

The bugs are red and black.
Where is my book?
I am so hot!

Add an end mark to each sentence.
What is your favorite book **?**
Watch out for that big snake **!**
I go to school **.**

— Sight Words —
Say each word. Trace it. Say the letter names.
walk   found   even

70 WRITING: Spelling and Grammar
Commas in a Series

You use a comma (,) to separate three or more words in a series.

I like to run, swim, and play soccer.

Add commas to these sentences.
We ate bread, cheese, and nuts.
I see dogs, cats, and rabbits.
Mom, Dad, and I went shopping.

— Sight Words —
Say each word. Trace it. Say the letter names.
family   like   buy

72 WRITING: Spelling and Grammar
Contractions

A **contraction** is a shortened way to write two words.
The letter or letters left out when putting together the two words are replaced by an apostrophe (').

I am = I'm   do not = don't
I have = I've   we will = we'll
he is = he's   let us = let's

I ɑm = I'm

Write the contraction for each word pair.
is not __isn't__   they will __they'll__
we have __we've__   she is __she's__
did not __didn't__   are not __aren't__
she will __she'll__   there is __there's__

— Sight Words —
Say each word. Trace it. Say the letter names.
some   which   just

74 VOCABULARY
Compound Words

Compound words are two or more words that together make a new word.
Often the meanings of the smaller words can help you figure out the meaning of the longer word.

snow + man = snowman
rain + bow = rainbow

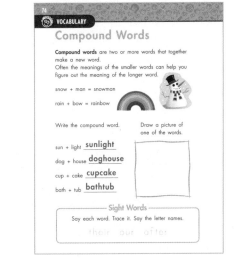

Write the compound word.   Draw a picture of one of the words.
sun + light __sunlight__
dog + house __doghouse__
cup + cake __cupcake__
bath + tub __bathtub__

— Sight Words —
Say each word. Trace it. Say the letter names.
their   our   after

76 VOCABULARY
Prefixes

A **prefix** is a word part added to the beginning of a word.
It changes the meaning of the word.

happy   **un**happy   (not happy)
read   **re**read   (read again)

Add **un** or **re** to finish each word.
un/re tie   **un/re** do
un/re make   **un** able

— Sight Words —
Say each word. Trace it. Say the letter names.
about   done   work

96

ANSWER KEY

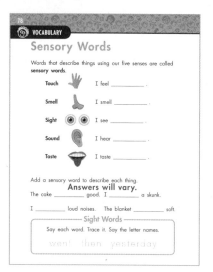

Sensory Words

Words that describe things using our five senses are called **sensory words**.

Touch	I feel _____ .
Smell	I smell _____ .
Sight	I see _____ .
Sound	I hear _____ .
Taste	I taste _____ .

Add a sensory word to describe each thing.
Answers will vary.
The cake _____ good. I _____ a skunk.

I _____ loud noises.   The blanket _____ soft.

— Sight Words —
Say each word. Trace it. Say the letter names.
went   then   yesterday

Shades of Meaning: Verbs

Verbs are action words. Some verbs mean almost the same thing. However, each verb has a slightly different meaning.

whisper   (talk quietly)
talk   (talk normally)
shout   (talk loudly)

Add a verb to finish each sentence: **ate, nibbled, gobbled.**

I **ate** my lunch. It was very good.

I **gobbled** down the cake. I was so hungry!

I **nibbled** on a piece of bread. I wasn't very hungry.

— Sight Words —
Say each word. Trace it. Say the letter names.
he's   for   must

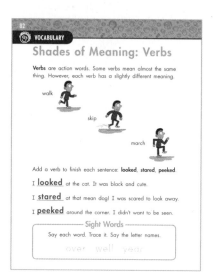

Shades of Meaning: Verbs

Verbs are action words. Some verbs mean almost the same thing. However, each verb has a slightly different meaning.

walk
skip
march

Add a verb to finish each sentence: **looked, stared, peeked.**

I **looked** at the cat. It was black and cute.

I **stared** at that mean dog! I was scared to look away.

I **peeked** around the corner. I didn't want to be seen.

— Sight Words —
Say each word. Trace it. Say the letter names.
over   well   year

Shades of Meaning: Adjectives

Adjectives are describing words. Some adjectives mean almost the same thing. However, each adjective has a slightly different meaning.

big   huge (very big)

Add an adjective to finish each sentence: **little, tiny.**

I see a **little** kitten. It is so cute!

Can you find the **tiny** pin? I can't see it.

— Sight Words —
Say each word. Trace it. Say the letter names.
away   out   think

Shades of Meaning: Adjectives

Adjectives are describing words. Some adjectives mean almost the same thing. However, each adjective has a slightly different meaning.

cold   freezing (very cold)

Add an adjective to finish each sentence: **pretty, beautiful.**

The butterfly is **pretty**.

That is the most **beautiful** butterfly in the world!

— Sight Words —
Say each word. Trace it. Say the letter names.
in   pretty   favorite

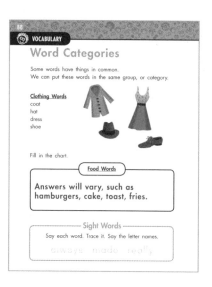

Word Categories

Some words have things in common. We can put these words in the same group, or category.

Clothing Words
coat
hat
dress
shoe

Fill in the chart.

Food Words
Answers will vary, such as hamburgers, cake, toast, fries.

— Sight Words —
Say each word. Trace it. Say the letter names.
always   made   really

Word Categories

Some words have things in common. We can put these words in the same group, or category.

Animal Words
bear
mouse
cat
snake

Fill in the chart.

Color Words
Answers will vary, such as red, orange, yellow, green, blue, purple, black, white.

— Sight Words —
Say each word. Trace it. Say the letter names.
any   head   special